UNBELIEVABLE...
BUT TRUE!

Real-Life Adventures
from the Files of
the Smithsonian Institution's
Center for
Short-Lived Phenomena

Written and Illustrated by JAMES CORNELL

SCHOLASTIC BOOK SERVICES
NEW YORK•TORONTO•LONDON•AUCKLAND•SYDNEY•TOKYO

Other Books by the Author
available from Scholastic Book Services
• FAKES FRAUDS & PHONIES
• MYTHICAL MONSTERS
• STRANGE SUDDEN & UNEXPECTED

Copyright © 1974 by James C. Cornell. All rights reserved. Published by Scholastic Book Services, a division of Scholastic Magazines, Inc.

15 14 13 12 11 10 9 8 7 6 5 4   7 8 9/7 01/8

Printed in the U.S.A.

06

Contents

A Word to the Reader: The World Watchers v

A Sleeping Giant Wakes 1

Diamonds from the Sky 5

The Antelope Invasion 8

The Slides of Death 11

Strange Tourists 14

The Cat and Mouse Caper 18

The Disappearing Pavement 21

The Bombarded Whales.................. 24

The Elk City Boulders 27

Moths on the Move 30

Fooling the Fishes 33

The Boiling Lake....................... 36

The Tale of the White-Tailed Rats 40

The December Giant 43

The Crawling Army 46

Chungar Has Disappeared 49

The Pesty Parakeets 52

The Rock in His Roof 55

Where Have All the Puffins Gone 58

Krakatoa Strikes Again 62

The Superbees of Brazil................. 65

Fire and Ice 68

Attack of the Killer Whales 72

Fire in the Lake 75

The Star-Struck Feline 79

The Poisoned Sheep 82

The Violent Birth 85

The Sad Saga of Suzie 88

The Slipping Earth 91

The Survivors 94

Stone Age Meets Space Age 98

The Falling Fishes 104

A Word to the Reader

The World Watchers

Millions of mice invade the grain fields of Australia, a diamond-studded meteorite falls on Finland, a volcano threatens to bury an island in Iceland...and one organization hears about them.

An African lava lake begins to boil over, antelope go on a rampage in Russia, Canadian bobcats invade Minnesota...and one organization takes immediate action.

Hungry beetles arrive in Samoa and start eating up the palm trees, army worms begin gnawing their way through Tanzania, South American parrots pester New York farmers...and one organization warns the world.

And what is that one extraordinary organization? It's the Smithsonian Institution's Center for Short-Lived Phenomena. Since 1968, the Center has kept its finger on the pulse of planet Earth, serving as the clearinghouse for news of all major biological, geophysical, and astrophysical events happening anywhere in the world.

Each year, the Center's hot line reports almost 200 events, including volcanos, earthquakes, fireballs, oil spills, industrial pollutions, flora blooms, animal migrations, bird kills, and a host of other exciting, unusual, and almost always strange occurrences.

News of these sudden and unexpected events is received at Center headquarters in Cambridge, Massachusetts, where it is immediately relayed by radio and cable to more than 2,000 scientists in 150 countries. Many of these scientists then rush to the scene of the event so they can observe and record the eruption, invasion, or infestation while it is still occurring.

The Center is the ultimate research tool of the modern age: an Early Warning System for science! More important, the Center provides the kind of global monitoring system necessary to protect our environment.

This book contains a number of the more exciting stories from the Center's files. Fantastic, incredible, even unbelievable, each one is true — a real-life episode in the continuing saga of Earth — this fantastic planet we call home.

— JC

A Sleeping Giant Wakes

An odd sound had awakened her in the middle of the long January night, and the housewife in the little village of Vestmannaeyjar on the island of Heimaey, Iceland, went downstairs for a predawn glass of warm milk. Just as she was about to return to bed, she saw a sight that would change her life forever.

1

The entire backyard of her home seemed on fire as red-hot liquid squirted out of the ground and flaming sky rockets shot up and over her house.

It was January 23, 1973, and the volcano Helgafell — dormant and silent for 7,000 years — had suddenly, violently, and incredibly awakened from its long sleep.

Since it forms the only above-water section of the Mid-Atlantic Ridge, Iceland is prone to all the stresses and strains usually found along the lines separating the earth's great crustal plates. Indeed, in this land of fire and ice, airplane flights over the volcanos are favorite tourist attractions.

The Helgafell eruption proved no tourist attraction, however. More like a nightmare, it sent fountains of burning lava spurting 300 feet in the air. Huge black cinders, some as big as baseballs, rained down on the island. A vile, eye-burning, throat-searing cloud of smoke and gas rose three miles high. A steady river of lava flowed down the mountain into the harbor. And the constant scream of escaping steam, punctuated every few seconds by deafening explosions, caused intense, ear-splitting pain.

The lava heated the harbor waters and threatened to block its mouth, but the real threat to Heimaey residents was suffocation under the tons of ash and cinders that fell in a steady black blizzard. Luckily the local fishing fleet was in port on the day of the disaster; and, within 24 hours, almost everyone was ferried to the mainland.

Observers arriving later saw a truly weird sight. With its street lamps still burning defiantly against the Arctic night, the deserted town of Vestmannaeyjar — once as bright and clean and modern as any American suburb — lay under a thick blanket of black. Only the tips of street signs poked above the 10-foot drifts of cinders. Some houses had collapsed under the weight; still others had burst into flames as the heat ignited oil storage tanks. And, looming over all, the fiery fountains of Helgafell continued to shoot skyward.

The eruption continued for several months, covering a three-square-mile area with lava and producing a central cone of lava more than 600 feet high. This cone, representing the new volcano spawned by the sleeping giant, was christened Kirkjufell, or "Church Hill."

The Kirkjufell eruption may be one of the best documented in history, with many observations made, some by orbiting satellites. Only the 1963 eruption of the nearby volcano Surtsey ever received such intensive scientific attention.

Ironically, in 1963, when the hordes of scientists and reporters came to Iceland to watch the birth of Surtsey, their jumping-off point was the

3

little village of Vestmannaeyjar and their transportation was the local fishing fleet. Now, many of these same observers had returned to witness the death of that village.

But Vestmannaeyjar would not die that easily. When, in July, the eruption finally stopped, the people of Heimaey Island returned to survey the damage and assess the chances for rebuilding their lives. Those chances looked slim: Tons of ash covered much of the island, molten lava still carpeted the ground, and smoke and steam continued to drift upward from cracks in the earth.

But the Icelanders are hardy people, long accustomed to the rigors of Arctic weather and the unpredictable nature of their violent land. They dug out their homes and salvaged whatever remained of their possessions. Then, with typical ingenuity and economy, the Icelanders turned the volcano's fury to their advantage.

They used the very cinders that had buried their buildings to pave new roads and airport runways. Then, they tapped the molten lava of the volcano itself to provide a cheap source of heat and power. By January 1974, one year after the first explosive yawns of that sleeping giant, new homes on Heimaey had been connected to water pipes heated by lava.

Diamonds from the Sky

Maybe Finnish farmer Tor-Erik Andersson had heard about "pennies from heaven," but he certainly never imagined that diamonds could fall from the skies.

Andersson was tending crops on his farm near Havero, Finland, one August day in 1971, when a loud and sudden noise rather like the combination of a jet plane and a thunderclap shattered the summer calm.

He could not think what had caused such a mysterious noise, especially on a fine clear day. But his nine-year-old son came running from another part of the farmyard screaming that something had just crashed into the roof of the storehouse.

The entire Andersson family ran to the small building. Throwing open the door, they found the one-room shack filled with dust that whirled upwards in a thin shaft of bright sunlight. The sunlight came through a small ragged hole in the tile roof overhead. On the floor, spotlighted by the sunbeam and almost directly beneath the hole in the roof, sat a small wooden box with a small hole in its cover.

Cautiously, they opened the box. Inside lay a dark gray rock about the size of a plum. The thin outer crust of the rock had cracked to reveal a concretelike interior.

Gingerly farmer Andersson picked up the rock. It was unusually heavy for its size — about three pounds — and Andersson guessed, correctly, that it must be a meteorite. This chunk of cosmic debris, perhaps the remains of a former asteroid, had traveled countless millions of miles in deep outer space before entering the atmosphere over Havero and finally falling through the roof of the storehouse and landing squarely inside this box.

However, an even more fantastic revelation was in store for the Anderssons — and scientists everywhere: Analysis of the rock showed that it contained traces of diamonds!

Diamonds found on earth are special carbon structures created by extremely high pressures deep within the ground. Diamonds found in meteorites, however, appear to result from the transformation of graphite (the lead used in "lead" pencils) by sudden shocks — perhaps the collision between the meteorite and other bodies in space. They are also extremely rare. Only six examples have been recorded since 1888.

Unfortunately, the Havero meteorite didn't make the Andersson family very rich, despite its valuable contents. The weight of the diamonds found in the meteorite was so small — it was, in fact, almost microscopic — as to make it essentially worthless. Tor-Erik Andersson would be the first to agree it is more profitable to raise grain than to try harvesting diamonds from the sky.

The Antelope Invasion

Sometimes man may be a little too protective.

Ten years ago, the Saiga Antelope, a deer native to Kazakhstan in central Russia, was reported on the verge of extinction. Russian environmentalists immediately adopted stricter hunting laws designed to save the antelope.

So successful was this protection plan that by

8

1965, the number of antelope had been restored to a half million. Unfortunately, that population continued to grow and grow...and grow! By 1971, it had risen to *one million* and was expected to double again in two years.

In such great numbers, the once-threatened species quickly turned into a tremendous pest.

The largest herd of antelope — some 800,000 strong — winter in the remote desert country of Bet Pak Dala far to the south of Kazakhstan. Great numbers of the animals usually die each winter from heavy snows and cold. Thousands survive, however, to migrate northward in the spring away from the killing heat and dryness of the desert summer.

Recently, however, the old migration patterns have changed. Instead of heading for their usual summer pastures, the antelope turn to the wheat fields of central Russia where they feast on the young shoots of the growing plants.

In addition to destroying these crops, the antelope also carry diseases that can infect domestic cattle and horses.

Soviet officials are experimenting with many techniques for protecting both the wheat and the antelope. For example, efforts have been made to drive off the antelope by buzzing them with low-flying airplanes. Unfortunately, the deer tend to return to the wheat fields as soon as the planes leave.

Some environmentalists have suggested fencing off food areas along the migration routes so that the deer may have enough to eat without relying on the wheat. Alas, this plan seems much too expensive.

In the end, there may be a return to old practices that once nearly wiped out the antelope. Russian farmers are clamoring for a relaxation of the game laws so the animals can once again be hunted.

The Slides of Death

One minute Dr. Liu Chen was sitting in his luxurious apartment overlooking the lights of Hong Kong harbor, the next minute he was picking himself out of a pile of rubble. Surrounded by the wreckage of his home and office, with the sounds of pain and dying ringing in his ears, the doctor considered himself lucky just to be alive.

Not so lucky were the more than 100 people killed and the other thousands left injured and homeless by massive landslides down the hills of Hong Kong following three days of torrential rains in June 1973.

Hong Kong, a small, conjested outcropping of rock connected to the mainland of China by a narrow neck, is one of the last British Crown Colonies: a strange outpost of capitalism in the communist world. Because Hong Kong represents some freedoms unknown on the mainland, its narrow streets are thronged with people and its steep hills are stacked with houses. Some of these houses are the fashionable and expensive homes of super-rich traders and merchants. More often, they are the shacks and shanties of the laborers, office workers, street vendors, and impoverished refugees who continue to pour into this city-state. But rich or poor, death recognized no class barriers when tons of rock and mud went hurtling down the hillsides.

The disaster was touched off by unusual weather conditions. More than 25 inches of rain fell on the city in less than three days. Storm drains became thundering waterfalls, roadways turned into swollen rivers, and low-lying areas became flooded lakes. Communication, transportation, and power lines were cut throughout the city.

Under this constant battering, the overloaded

slopes could hold no longer. In one of the worst slides, in the Kwuntong District, a huge section of hillside, 150 feet high and 600 feet wide, plummeted into a cluster of shanty-town huts housing some 400 people.

The other major landslide occurred in the more exclusive district of Victoria Peak, where apartment houses perch on rocky ledges above the harbor. Here, an apartment building near the top of the slope collapsed. As it fell, it smashed into a second structure which, in turn, hit a third and then a fourth. Like giant dominoes, the buildings toppled over in a horrible chain reaction.

On the fourth day, the rains ended. But their toll was enormous. Since the destruction had cut across economic lines, both rich and poor mourned their losses.

Strange Tourists

Japanese seaweed is bobbing in the surf off England. African fish are basking in the Florida sunshine. Tahitian beetles are bugging Samoa. And Chinese clams are clogging drains in Pennsylvania.

The Jet Set is not limited to human beings.

Scores of exotic plants and animals are circling the globe — some carried as stowaways on planes and boats and others deliberately carted along in the baggage of unthinking tourists and well-meaning scientists.

Unfortunately, some of these foreign visitors find their new homes so pleasant that they have taken root — with disastrous results. Carried to an environment where they have no natural enemies or diseases, the strange tourists multiply at abnormal rates and crowd out the native stock.

For example, in 1973 British biologists found Japanese seaweed growing along England's southern coastline.

Perhaps the seaweed arrived wrapped around the anchor chain of a Japanese ship. No one knows. But one thing is certain: The new breed of oriental weed is crowding out the local species. Allowed to grow unchecked, it could change the ecology of the English coastal flats.

Similarly, a nasty little beetle has found its way to American Samoa aboard oil tankers sailing from Tahiti. Well-known in other parts of the South Pacific, this beetle is a major destroyer of palm trees.

The beetle lays its eggs between the tightly rolled folds of sprouting leaves. When the eggs hatch, the beetle larvae (or worm stage) feed on the leaves, causing them to turn brown. Young palms that lose too many leaves soon wither and die.

In the American South, some popular pets have turned into ecological time bombs. Fresh-water species of imported tropical fish have found their way into Florida's inland lakes and rivers, dumped there from home aquariums or "fish farms."

A fish called the "black acara," for instance, has felt so at home that it now makes up 80 percent of the population in many waterways. The "blue tilapia," an African version of the sunfish, was actually brought to Florida on purpose because scientists thought it would eat up harmful plant growth in the canals. The blue fish ate up the vegetation, all right, but it also drove out all the other native fish.

The Chinese clam is another foreign creature taking over American waters. No one knows how the Chinese clams arrived in the United States, but they were first spotted on the West Coast in 1938. (Maybe travelers from the Orient brought back a few as snacks and released them in rivers instead.) Now, 35 years later, the pesty clams have shown up in the East Coast rivers.

The small, gray, fresh-water bivalve multiplies at a phenomenal rate. Since it has no natural enemies, the population of clams in some areas has grown so large that they clog water valves and sewage drains, foul riverbeds, and crowd out other water life.

Actually, the clam problem could be solved — simply by eating them! The tiny shellfish is considered quite a delicacy in Asia; perhaps they will soon find a spot on American menus.

The Cat and Mouse Caper

Invasion! Invasion!

In 1972, two very different parts of the world faced invasions by two very different kinds of animals! Unusually large numbers of a wildcat known as the Canadian lynx were seen slipping over the border into Minnesota and other northern states. And, halfway around the world, in

Queensland, Australia, millions of mice overran farms, fields, and houses.

The reason for the invasions: population explosion.

For example, the Canadian lynx — a scrappy little wildcat noted for the long tufts of hair on its eartips — is normally rare south of the Canadian border. However, in the winter of 1972, scores of lynx were spotted throughout Minnesota, North Dakota, and other neighboring states.

Wildlife experts suspect these wandering wildcats were pushed south by overcrowding in the Canadian north woods. With their normal hunting grounds stripped clean by a population explosion, the lynx may have headed south in search of new sources of food.

Most of the lynx shot or captured seemed to be in good health, with strong, hard, unworn teeth. Moreover, the roaming lynx seemed relatively unafraid of human beings. All this suggested that the cats had spent most of their lives in the wilderness.

The visiting lynx were particularly bold — hunting openly aroun barnyards and even suburban backyards. Unfortunately for farmers and homeowners, the wildcat will eat almost anything it can kill, including house pets and poultry.

At the same time, farmers in Australia were facing a similar crisis. For the second year in a row, hordes of hungry mice had invaded the grainfields of Queensland.

The common house mouse, although small in size, poses a giant problem for the Australians. Periodically, the population of these mice explodes and they overrun fields and farms. In 1972, the mice became a plague. Millions of the gluttonous rodents ate their way over the land, chewing up much of the winter wheat crop. Then they turned to the summer crops such as sunflowers and sorghum. Finally, they nibbled their way into stored crops at granaries and mills.

How to counteract these "invasions" on opposite sides of the globe? No one has come up with viable solutions but one suggestion — made jokingly, of course — was that the cat and mouse problem could be solved simply by sending the Canadian lynx to Australia!

The Disappearing Pavement

Late one winter night in 1973, a young man and his date, both residents of Swansea, Wales, were driving home from a party at a friend's house. The night was clear and surprisingly mild for January. The party had been fun, the food and drink delicious, and the couple was in fine spirits.

Then the road disappeared!

Suddenly a pleasant drive had turned into a nightmare. As the front end of the car lurched forward into apparent nothingness, the panic-striken driver slammed on his brakes. The car skidded, its underframe scraped the ground, and then, miraculously, the back wheels caught on solid pavement. The car stopped with a sickening seesaw motion, its headlights pointing downward into a deep black chasm.

The couple sat stunned for several minutes. Terrified that any false move might send the car toppling into this bottomless pit, they edged toward the doors and carefully opened the latches. Then, together they jumped from the car and ran back down the road away from the gaping gulf.

Once calm, the couple ventured back to the car and the hole in the road to see what had happened. They found their car on the brink of a huge pit nearly 20 feet wide and 30 feet deep. They were baffled.

The police arrived shortly after and pulled the car from the edge of the hole, roping off a section of the highway in case of further collapse. But they too were puzzled by this strange phenomenon. What had caused the pavement to disappear in Swansea?

The mystery was cleared up soon, with the arrival of geologists — and officials from the National Mining Commission. The pavement on the Swansea road didn't really disappear, it fell into an old air shaft that had ventilated a mine abandoned some 50 years before.

Local residents remembered that 16 years earlier a similar collapse had occurred a mile away. That collapse, too, had been into an old lost mine.

Swansea is undercut with miles and miles of unused coal-mine tunnels. Many of these mines closed so long ago that no one even knows where they lead. As the modern city of Swansea developed, homes and roads and shopping centers have been built over these lost mines. Today, the entire city sits on a honeycombed substrata that seems ready to collapse at any moment.

Perhaps the rest of Swansea may one day suddenly disappear into a huge deep pit!

The Bombarded Whales

From the Bible to modern novels, the whale has served as the universal symbol of massive power, frightening strength, and monumental size.

Many scientists also think the great sea mammals — the whales and their cousins, the porpoises — may be the most intelligent nonhuman creatures alive. Indeed, some experts claim the minds of the whale and porpoise are more like that of man than any other animal.

Nothing, then, is more sad and sickening than to see these deep sea monarchs lying helpless and dying on a dry beach.

Yet, each year, the Smithsonian Center for Short-Lived Phenomena receives scores of reports of whales running aground on shallow sandbars and beaches to perish high and dry in the sun.

One of the strangest cases of beached whales was reported in February 1971, when some three dozen giant sperm whales rammed themselves into the sand at Gunnamatta Beach near Melbourne, Australia.

The shocking picture of these animals spread out like some discarded black blimps produced outcries of dismay and anger. Especially when the tragic reasons for the beaching became known.

Whales travel in herds, just like cattle, elephants, or tribes of men. Led by an old bull, or chief, they respond to group pressures and instincts.

Whales also communicate with each other, as well as navigate through the water, by means of a sophisticated natural sonar system. They send out high-pitched beeping noises that bounce off obstacles and objects underwater, such as reefs and sand shoals, to help them negotiate the murky depths. The system works best in deep water.

At Gunnamatta Beach this intricate sonar system may have been confused by man.

Two days before the whales were found on the beach, a naval installation about nine miles east of Gunnamatta held gunnery practice for several hours in the morning.

Scores of anti-aircraft practice shells were fired over the ocean to explode above the water's surface.

Since the shells didn't detonate in the water, it is unlikely that any of the whales were physically harmed. However, the air bursts may have caused shock waves damaging to their sonar systems.

Even more likely, the sound of the explosions may have so frightened the whales that they became panicky and confused. Losing their direction in the surf, the whales probably swam into the shallow waters near the coast by mistake. Once in shallow waters, their sonar would become totally useless. Perhaps they then rushed onto the beach in a suicidal frenzy to escape the sound of the explosions — and their own fright.

The Elk City Boulders

"Galloping granite! Call the sheriff! The Fire Department and the National Guard too! There's big boulders sprouting up in the back forty!"

The residents of Elk City, Oklahoma, surely were shocked in the spring of 1973 to see huge boulders suddenly pop out of the ground in the middle of Jim Walker's pasture.

The rocks, all red shale, tore through the bed of a small creek crossing Walker's ranch and created a natural version of Stonehenge: a wall-like formation of tall jagged stones, some standing 20 feet high and weighing as much as 30 tons.

In addition, a host of smaller boulders were strewn over an area 230 feet long and 100 feet wide. A network of deep narrow crevices spread outward from the rocks. Many trees and shrubs were uprooted and toppled by the force of the boulder upheaval.

Scientists from the Oklahoma Geological Survey arrived on the scene the next day. The puzzled experts attempted to explain why these mysterious monoliths were now jutting from the normally flat and gentle grazing land.

They ruled out the possibility of a giant meteorite impact, or of a volcanic eruption, or even of an earthquake along existing fault lines. Instead, the geologists felt the boulder uplift was probably caused by the nonexplosive buildup of pressure from propane gas — the same gas used to heat homes.

Oklahoma is a major producer of fossil fuels, including oil and natural gas. In 1953, one of the large oil companies drilled a well just 2,000 feet north of the now boulder-strewn pasture. This well bottomed out at about 1,300 feet in a salt bed. The oil company then turned the dry shaft into an underground storage tank for liquid petroleum gas, or propane.

Apparently for the next 10 years, propane gas had slowly leaked through the well-casing into the surrounding rocks. Finally the pressure became so great it caused expansion and uplifting of the shale levels.

Man's interference with the earth's natural order had resulted in an unusual and totally unexpected geological disturbance, causing Jim Walker's quiet pasture to be turned into a giant rockpile.

Moths on the Move

Unbelievable sights are commonplace in the tropics. Nature seems to conjure up its wildest magic in the steamy regions around the equator. Here the combination of intense sun and extreme moisture produces the biggest, brightest, and often most beautiful of nature's plants, animals, and insects. Yet, even the long-time residents of the tropics are sometimes thrilled and surprised by one of nature's more spectacular shows.

For example, during one week in August 1969, the residents of Panama City were bedazzled by the appearance of millions of green and black "butterflies." The skies were literally filled throughout the day with these magnificent creatures as they migrated across the city.

According to scientists at the Smithsonian's Tropical Research Institute in the Canal Zone, these beautiful "butterflies" were actually moths. Known formally as the *Urania fulgens*, the moth is closely related to the well-known "Green Page" species found in Trinidad.

Some sort of moth migration occurs almost every year in Panama, with the insects moving west in the dry season and back east again in the rainy season.

Thus, the moth migration of 1969 was not unique. But few people could ever remember having seen so many of the "butterflies" before. Apparently, the previous year's weather had provided a particularly good breeding season. The multitude of moths was the product of another natural population explosion.

As far as biologists could determine, however, this was one population explosion that caused no one any grief. Just the opposite. The moths put on a great show for those people who just like to sit back and watch nature fly by.

The moths only flew during the day, so they were particularly visible. Apparently they navigate by the sun, so the sky was dense with moths each dawn as huge flocks took off for their day's flight.

These moths are unusually strong fliers. They cruise along at a rate of about eight miles an hour, so they can cross Panama from end to end in about a week. Moreover, they can cross mountains and even wide stretches of open sea with ease.

Because they are so strong, the moths easily avoid most dangerous obstacles, including collectors' nets. And they don't seem to have any natural enemies. Most birds don't even try to eat them.

If the moths faced any hazard on their journey across Panama, it was from man's own greatest menace in this modern age — the automobile! During the week of their migration, thousands (maybe millions) of moths met squishy deaths against windshields, headlights, and radiator grills.

But at least in death the moths had their revenge: Traffic was tied up all over Panama, as irate drivers were forced out of their cars to clean green and black wings from their windshields.

Fooling the Fishes

On the morning of January 28, 1971, thousands of the fish known as "mossbunkers" mysteriously died in Oyster Creek, New Jersey, about 60 miles south of New York City.

Because a large nuclear power plant operates on Oyster Creek, investigators from the Environmental Protection Agency hurried to the scene to see if the fish kill was somehow connected with the leakage of deadly radioactive wastes from the plant. The findings of the investigation were startling. The power plant *did* cause the deaths of the fish. But not by radiation poisoning. Or explosions. Or leakage of waste materials into the water. The poor unsuspecting fish were the victims of *thermal shock*, an unusual and unexpected danger from atomic plants that may be impossible to prevent.

Their first clue to the mystery of the dead fish came when investigators learned that because of mechanical problems the plant had shut down operations on January 27.

Normally, one would think shutting down an atomic generating plant might protect, rather than harm, fish. Not so, unfortunately, in this case. The dead fish were discovered downstream the next day.

For two years, the Oyster Creek plant had drawn some 450,000 gallons of water per minute from Barnegat Bay to cool the steam created by the atomic reactor system. After it was used as a coolant, the water was dumped back into Oyster Creek, a tributary of the bay.

But this recirculated water was now *15 to 20 degrees hotter*. As a result, in the middle of winter, Oyster Creek became a warm, mild stream.

The dead fish found in Oyster Creek after the

plant shut down were warm water species. Mossbunkers usually cannot stand the cold New Jersey waters and migrate south to the warmer waters off the North Carolina coast each winter.

Since the heated waters discharged by the atomic cooling system created springlike temperatures in Oyster Creek all year long, the mossbunkers were unaware that the seasons were changing and they remained in the north after summer ended.

When the atomic plant shut down, the water temperature suddenly dropped 22 degrees. Overnight the creek returned to its normal winter conditions.

Unprotected and unprepared for this rapid arrival of winter, the mossbunkers became the victims of "thermal shock." The sudden cold snap literally jolted their bodily functions to a standstill.

The Oyster Creek fish kill underlines still another danger associated with atomic energy plants. For many years, environmentalists have been concerned about the effects of heating on marine biology and plants. Not many people have considered the reverse situation: What happens when the unnatural heat supply is turned off? How many more fish will die after being fooled into thinking it is June in January?

The Boiling Lake

For most winter-weary North Americans, the blue Caribbean is a tropical playground of tiny islands where one finds the warmth of the sun. One of those islands, St. Vincent, is among the last green pearls in the long necklace that stretches south from Puerto Rico to Trinidad. St. Vincent is a lush world of quiet lagoons and beautiful beaches.

Towering over this peaceful Caribbean hideaway is the Soufriere Volcano. The 1902 eruption of Soufriere caused widespread destruction. Since then, the volcano has lain still. In fact, Soufriere has remained so inactive that a deep, dark mountain lake formed in its crater.

But in the fall of 1971, people came down the mountains of St. Vincent with reports of strange things happening high in the Soufriere crater. The lake had changed color and some unknown and unseen turbulence was churning up the surface.

When scientists climbed to the crater rim, they found the surface of the lake half obscured by mists and vapors. Occasionally, an updraft lifted the warm and wettish vapors to the rim, engulfing the men in a foul-smelling mist.

There could be no mistake. A large heat source — most likely molten rock — had pushed up from the lake floor. Steam or hot lava blowing through the cracks in the lake bed was heating the water. Soufriere was showing the first signs of a major eruption!

Within the next few days, the scientists made the long descent into the crater. At the bottom, they found that the water level had recently risen, drowning the plants and smaller trees along the steep-sided shore. The water of the crater lake was warm to the touch, yellowish-brown to the eye, and sulphurous to the nose.

While apparently smooth and calm, the entire surface seemed to be steaming — with vapor rising as steady and as thick as one of those old-time London fogs.

Most amazing, the scientists found a brand new island sitting in the center of the lake! This island — made up of approximately a dozen large blocks of black rock — represented the top-most part of a dome-shaped lava mass that had been slowly seeping through the floor of the lake for more than a month.

In the next two months, this rocky island rose some 30 feet above the lake's surface, spreading 1,000 feet long and 300 feet wide.

Although the threat of a violent eruption remained very real, the absence of any unusual or strong earthquake activity greatly reduced the chances of a major disaster.

So confident of Soufriere's safety were two of the scientists that they rowed out into the middle of the steaming lake to plant an earthquake monitor on the island itself. As they neared the pile of hot rocks, they found the water getting progressively warmer. Indeed, at the very edge of the island, where water directly contacted the emerging lava, the lake was literally boiling! The scientists dropped off their instrumets and rowed quickly back to the crater rim.

The Soufriere crater bubbled for a few months more and then returned to its usual dormant state. St. Vincent had been spared a repeat of the terrible 1902 eruption. Of course, now this little island in the sun had its own little island nestling in the mouth of the Soufriere Volcano. However, it is one Caribbean isle that will attract few tourists.

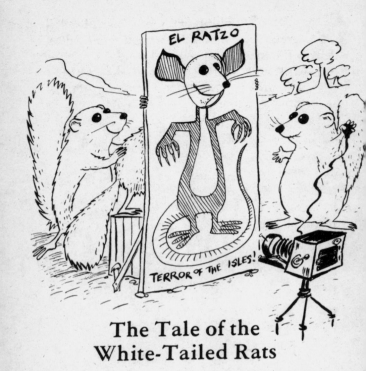

The Tale of the
White-Tailed Rats

The reports sounded terrifying: Thousands of rampaging rats had invaded the island of Formentera in the Mediterranean. Or had they? The true tale of the white-tailed rat invasion apparently depended on who was telling it.

According to angry and excited farmers on this tiny island off the coast of Spain, hordes of hungry rats were eating their way through vegetable, grain, and fruit crops and threatening to destroy the island's entire food supply.

On the other hand, calmer and cooler scientific experts claimed there was no "invasion," the number of rodents was not unusual, there was little or no damage to food supplies, and, indeed, *the rats really were not even rats*!

First reports of the so-called rat invasion reached the Smithsonian Center in late December 1971, when Formentera farmers requested government help in combating an apparent plague of white-tailed rodents.

The Spanish government took no immediate action, but it did ask zoologists from the University of Barcelona to investigate the situation on Formentera. The island is part of the Balearic chain, a string of green jewels off Spain's Costa del Sol which attracts thousands of tourists yearly. A rat plague would be disastrous, especially if it spread to the popular island resorts of Mallorca and Ibiza.

Fortunately, the scientists found little cause for alarm. First, the rodents in question turned out to be a special breed of garden dormouse with long, white tails and an equally long Latin name (*Eliomys quercinus ophisuae*) that lives only on Formentera.

Because the squirrel-like dormouse is unique

to Formentera, it obviously couldn't be "invading" from somewhere else.

Moreover, zoologists claim even the hungriest dormice seldom dine on farm crops. Their normal diet consists of small animals such as lizards and other mice, occasionally spiced with spiders, beetles, and assorted insects.

A bumper crop of little white-tailed dormice the previous year may have produced a minor population explosion when the rodents awoke from hibernation, convincing farmers an "invasion" was underway. More likely, the farmers of Formentera were looking for some government aid and the reports of "severe crop damage" could have been exaggerations designed to gain sympathy for their cause.

No steps were taken to exterminate the rodents. Government officials — at the suggestion of zoologists — wisely decided that any attempts to eliminate the dormice would only upset the island's delicate ecological balance.

The saga of the white-tailed rodents isn't over yet, of course. As long as there are both farmers and dormice in Formentera, there will be new chapters written in this long-running tale of long-tailed rodents.

The December Giant

The loud rumble and accompanying tremor felt like a minor earthquake as it rolled over the small farm near Montevallo, Alabama. Windows rattled, doors swung open, and a few dishes crashed onto the floor. The farmer's wife ran out into the cool December afternoon, certain her modest frame house would soon collapse around her. But the "quake" ended as quickly as it had begun. No sounds or shakes followed. The woman returned to her house and promptly forgot the incident — until three months later!

Early the next spring, two hunters tramping through dense woods near this central Alabama town stumbled on — and nearly fell into — a giant sinkhole more than 400 feet wide and 150 feet deep.

Apparently it was the collapse of the earth's upper layers into this hole that caused the considerable shaking felt by the farmer's wife.

Dubbed the "December Giant" by geologists, this massive sinkhole is thought to be the largest ever formed in the United States.

Sinkholes are natural features in those areas of the country with limestone substrata, and they occur when topsoil and subsurface clays collapse into underground caverns. In the past, sinkholes of this sort have caused serious damage to highways, railroads, sewage facilities, homes, and other buildings. At least 1,000 sinkholes as well as other land "slips" and crackings have occurred during the past 15 years within the same 10-square-mile area of Shelby County, Alabama.

Collapse may be triggered by a variety of natural factors, but many geologists feel man's overuse of the land is the main reason for the increasing creation of sinkholes. The unrestricted construction of homes, apartments, and shopping centers in areas with limited water supplies tends to drain off the water normally trapped in the ground. As this water supply drops, the natural support of the underground caves decreases and the delicate clay structure near the surface of the earth loses its support. Also, with the water content of the ground lowered, rain and melting snow soaks rapidly through the clay, thus weakening it even more. Overloading the surface with buildings and roads and straining the structure by the steady vibrations of factory operations and heavy traffic further weakens the earth. Eventually, the earth's various layers fall apart and huge sections of the ground suddenly disappear beneath the surface in the swoosh of a collapsing sinkhole.

State and federal geologists recently began a program to map and monitor the potential sinkholes of central and northern Alabama. The program includes remote sensing equipment carried aboard airplanes and the possible use of observation systems on orbiting spacecraft.

The geologists hope to spot the next potential collapse, so some future "giant" won't gobble up an entire city.

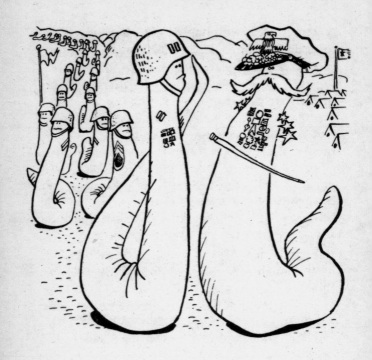

The Crawling Army

A silent force of deadly killers were creeping stealthily into Tanzania, and government officials immediately launched an all-out counteroffensive to control and contain the invaders.

Tribal hunters on the warpath? Guerrilla infiltrators? Revolutionary insurgents?

No, not quite. The enemy attacking the croplands of this East African country was the common *army worm*, a destructive force more feared by farmers than any political or military foe.

This squiggly, wiggly horde of hungry soldiers ate its way from southern Kenya into northern Tanzania during early 1971, destroying grassy pastures and valuable fields of maize, sorghum, and rice as it moved south.

The army worm actually is the yellow-gray larva of a moth known to gardeners almost everywhere as a *giant pest*! In its worm, or caterpillar, stage, the insect travels in large bands, feasts on green plants, and generally makes life miserable for farmers.

Although army worm "invasions," or, more precisely, infestations, occur annually in East Africa between November and May, this would be one of the worst.

The army worms chewed up grasses and grains all along the Kenya-Tanzania border, from Kilimanjaro to Karatu. Scattered outbreaks even threatened plant life in the world-famous Serengeti National Park. Rice and sorghum fields attacked by the worms were totally destroyed.

By lucky chance, many farmers had not yet planted their crops at the time of the worm invasion, and thus were spared from almost certain ruin. Still, almost 10,000 square miles were infested, with the insects numbering in the many,

many millions! In some areas of the country, observers counted more than 100 worms per square foot!

Fortunately, the voracious caterpillars were confined to the grazing pastures of the northern borders. However, new outbreaks usually follow the migratory paths of the adult moth, springing up later in the places where eggs are dropped.

To brace for future onslaughts of this strange army that literally travels on its stomach, East African officials now maintain special "worm watches," so counterattacks can be launched immediately against new outbreaks of the pest. Long-range "worm warnings" are issued to edgy farmers armed with pesticides. If the worms can be stopped before they mature as moths and reproduce again, major disasters — and possible famines — may be averted.

Chungar Has Disappeared

The tough Indian miners who burrow deep beneath the rugged Andes Mountains of Peru know the hardship and pain of scratching out small wages at a backbreaking task. They know, too, the terror of living with the constant threat of sudden, unexpected, and violent death.

At noon on March 18, 1971, that threat became a reality for the miners of Chungar, a bleak mining settlement northeast of Lima, the capital. A massive mudslide, triggered by a minor earthquake, literally wiped Chungar from the face of the earth.

The slide killed more than 1,000 men, women, and children, including the entire student body of a school swept away in the wild rush of water, mud, and rocks.

The disaster went generally unnoticed in Lima, where few people worried over the slight earth tremor that shook their city. Tradesmen continued their business, housewives finished preparing their large midday meals, and school children completed their morning lessons. After all, why should they be alarmed? Peru experiences as many as 1,500 earth tremors a year.

The towering Andes Mountains, which form the snow-capped backbone of Peru and separate the cosmopolitan Spanish coast from the wild Indian interior, are young, growing mountains still in the throes of evolutionary change.

As these "geologically immature" mountains push up out of the earth, they cause quakes, tremors, soil cracks, landslides, and a host of other violent surface changes.

While the people in Lima felt the tremor and perhaps said a silent prayer before returning to their daily activities, the poor miners of Chungar needed much more than prayers to save them.

Several weeks of torrential rains before the earthquake had loosened boulders and rock formations high above Chungar on the steep and barren mountainsides. The final jolt of the earthquake sent huge hunks of the mountain rolling down the slopes and into a deep mountain lake known as Yanahuay Lagoon.

As the dirt and debris splashed into the lake, the water level rose dramatically, overflowing the banks and flooding into the streets, homes, and mine shafts of Chungar — and sweeping away cars, trucks, livestock, and human bodies.

Chungar and its inhabitants virtually disappeared beneath an ugly brown river of mud.

The Pesty Parakeets

The New York businessman gazed out of his office window and saw a sight he could hardly believe. In the middle of winter, there on the window ledge, sat a small gray parrot!

The monk parakeet, a tropical native, has found a new home in North America. Worse yet, this one-time harmless household pet for thousands of Americans has turned into a major pest that threatens to upset the already delicate ecology balance of the urbanized East Coast.

This chattering little bird, with gray plumage vaguely resembling a friar's hood, has long been the scourge of farmers throughout South America. Yet, despite its bad reputation, between 1968 and 1972 more than 50,000 birds were imported into the United States as pets.

Some of these birds escaped or were released, and now small parakeet colonies have become established in New York, New Jersey, and Connecticut. And sightings of the monk parakeets have been reported from over 20 other states, ranging from North Dakota to Arizona.

Several hundred of the birds are estimated to be living wild in New York City alone. Although usually found in subtropical regions of South America, the birds can apparently survive winter temperatures as low as zero degrees by building nests in the warm sheltered nooks and crannies provided by a modern city.

Flocks of birds in the countryside may also build large communal nests of sticks in which they live. Most of the nest sites are built close to fruit trees, such as wild cherry, apple, and mulberry. The nests themselves are built from the twigs of these trees and are woven together to produce a large dwelling with one or more entrance tunnels located on the lower side of the nest.

Usually the nests are built in the eaves of buildings or on telephone poles and trees between 20 and 30 feet from the ground. These nests are often located on a hill or in an open area to allow for observation of approaching danger.

No monk parakeets have been imported to the United States since 1972 when the Department of Agriculture placed a ban on the importation of all exotic birds.

Some experts think this ban may cause the decline of the birds; but others are not so optimistic. No natural diseases or parasites seem to affect the birds in North America.

In their native habitat of Argentina, Bolivia, Brazil, Uruguay, and Paraguay, the parakeets are major agricultural pests, destroying thousands of dollars worth of corn, millet, sorghum, and other grains, as well as citrus fruits, each year. Worse news: The Argentine government has tried to wipe out the birds since 1947 — by every means possible — and nothing yet has worked!

The Rock in His Roof

Just before dawn on April 8, 1971, an early-rising resident of West Hartford, Connecticut, looked out her window and saw "a bright streak of light like a rocket bursting in the air!" A long dark trail like that from a jet aircraft remained above the horizon for several minutes.

About an hour later, the alarm rang in the

home of Paul Cassarino in nearby Wethersfield. Mr. Cassarino, who was a machinist at America's last horseshoe nail factory, awakened and walked from the bedroom into the living room of his second-floor apartment. He immediately noticed something odd. A small pile of plaster and dust lay in the center of the carpet.

Angered because he had just paid to have his ceiling plastered, he looked up to see what had happened to the new work.

His mouth dropped open with surprise and he nearly toppled over backwards.

There, poking out of the middle of his smooth white plastered ceiling, was a small black rock.

Mr. Cassarino climbed onto an armchair and with the blade of his penknife pried the stone loose. It was about three inches in diameter and unusually heavy. By squinting up through the hole in the plaster, he could see there was also a hole in the fiberglass insulation material between the ceiling eaves, and still another hole through the boards and asbestos tiles of the roof itself.

Whatever this strange object was — it had fallen out of the sky! Mr. Cassarino called the police.

The police — plus the fire department and several assorted reporters — arrived at his home almost immediately. Not one of them could offer a reasonable explanation for the rock that had torn through his roof. Luckily, someone else also heard about this strange event: a local astronomer, who stopped by that same morning to survey the stone.

The astronomer's answer was fast and to the point! Mr. Cassarino's house had been hit by a meteorite — a piece of outer-space material that had entered the atmosphere and crashed through the roof with the last remaining force of its fall. It was probably the same object that had been seen over Hartford as a "bursting rocket" earlier that morning.

The 12.3-ounce stone, now known as the Wethersfield Meteorite, was only the eleventh in the past century known to have struck a building.

Luckily, scientists anxious to receive samples of the meteorite for analysis and study provided Mr. Cassarino with enough money to fix his roof.

Where Have All
the Puffins Gone

The puffin, a large rotund diving bird that paddles about the cold northern Atlantic seas, seems doomed to the same fate as the dodo — *extinction*!

Reports from professional and amateur bird watchers in the Hebrides Islands near the west coast of Scotland indicate the puffin population is rapidly and mysteriously declining.

At one time, millions upon millions of puffins — the smallest member of the auk family and a northern version of the penguin — ranged the waters from Brittany to Norway. Even as late as 1960, some three million pairs of puffins roosted in the craggy rock islands jutting from the sea west of Scotland.

Ten years ago, the mile-long island of Dun was riddled with puffin burrows, or nests. But by 1969, only half the island was covered with nesting birds.

Then in 1972, a bird census by British officials indicated that Dun's puffin population, once in the millions, had now been reduced to about 250,000 birds.

The cause of this rapid puffin decline is a mystery. All possible reasons have been investigated — attacks by rats, seagulls, and man; food shortages; breeding failures; epidemic disease; even oil pollution — but none are the likely killers. However, in winter the puffins migrate to distant and little-watched waters where they may be tangling with poisonous materials dumped in the water by man.

Professional bird watchers urge that worldwide efforts be made to investigate the puffin decline and its possible causes. If the answers aren't found soon, they fear the puffin may join the long and tragic list of extinct birds.

Some 161 species of birds have disappeared

since 1600, with 54 species lost in this century alone. Most of these missing birds, such as the American passenger pigeon and the heath hen, have been the victims of man.

The classic victim was the dodo, a big lovable bird that could neither fly nor swim and died because of its trusting nature.

The dodo lived on the island of Mauritius in the Indian Ocean. With only rudimentary wings and no swimming ability, the two-foot-tall dodo apparently came to the island aboard logs that had drifted out to sea. On Mauritius, without any natural enemies or diseases, they multiplied and prospered until the first explorers arrived in the early 1600's.

Gentle, curious, and trusting, the dodos waddled down to the beach to look at the strange two-legged creatures and were immediately clubbed over the head and either roasted for dinner or cut up as fish bait. (The apparent willingness of the dodo to submit to its own slaughter gave rise to the phrase "dumb as a dodo.")

Those dodos that somehow escaped the cooking pots soon fell victim to the many diseases brought ashore by the sheep, goats, and rats carried on the visiting ships. Long-removed from the mainland, the dodos had lost any natural immunity to the diseases of the outside world. The last dodo on earth died in 1681.

The puffin at least can fly — in a sense. Although smaller than the dodo, the puffin shares certain features with its extinct cousins — an oversized body and undersized wings. In fact, the puffin is so disproportionately built it cannot take off from a standing start. Instead, the clumsy bird must launch itself by jumping from a high rock or cliff.

While this lumbering flight allows the puffin to escape enemies such as seagulls, rats, and men, some other unknown and deadly form of killer is reducing the puffin flocks. The number of newly hatched puffins — little round fluffy balls that resemble chirping cream puffs — is declining yearly. Unless someone can discover — and stop — the cause of their decline, the puffin may join the dodo. Gone forever!

Krakatoa Strikes Again

When the volcano Krakatoa blows its top, the whole world seems to hear about it. The small volcanic island in the Sunda Strait between Sumatra and Java erupted in August 1883 with the greatest natural display of raw power and destructive fury ever recorded in modern history.

The tremendous force of the volcanic eruption

completely disintegrated most of the island and permanently altered the shape of the strait. As the old volcanic cone split apart, red-hot lava and incandescent boulders poured into the surrounding waters and turned the sea into a boiling, bubbling broth.

A large portion of the sea floor collapsed, creating a series of towering tidal waves that capsized boats of every size and description and flooded low coastal areas in minutes, killing thousands of sailors, fishermen, and their families.

The sound of the explosion, perhaps the loudest noise ever heard, resounded throughout Indonesia, the Philippines, and, unbelievably enough, as far away as Japan and Australia.

The volume of ash and smoke released by Krakatoa was so great that the sky turned black at midday and hunks of volcanic debris were scattered across the Indian Ocean from Ceylon to Madagascar.

One massive cloud of dust particles was carried high into the upper atmosphere and circled the earth three times, creating brilliant sunsets in Europe and North America for more than a year after the eruption.

While nothing could compare with the dramatic and devastating events of 1883, Krakatoa erupted again in 1972. And, again, much of the world felt the aftereffects.

On April 11, a crewman aboard a Scottish freighter bound for Djakarta spotted what seemed to be extremely high waves breaking against the southern shore of Krakatoa. Closer inspection revealed that an underwater eruption was churning up the coastal waters into a turbulent, steamy froth.

Thin lines of smoke seeped from cracks in the mountainside near the old volcanic peak, and a spray of fine white ash had settled over the southwestern side of the mountain.

Throughout the next few months, similar activity could be observed at Krakatoa. Thunderlike rumblings could be heard and puffs of dirty white ash rose high in the air. At night, angry red streaks of flame shot through the murky clouds of smoke and dust.

In early September, weather observers on islands throughout the Western Pacific reported unusually high levels of smoke and haze that persisted for many days. In both the Caroline and Marshall Islands, visibility was down to three miles — extremely poor conditions for lands traditionally sunny and clear.

The darkening clouds drifted over the Pacific on southwesterly breezes, indicating to many meteorologists that the strange source of pollution in paradise must have been that old scourge of the Sunda Strait again — the Krakatoa volcano!

The Superbees of Brazil

Hide your honey pots! Lock your doors, close your windows! Get out the leather gloves and protective goggles! The Brazilian Superbees are headed north!

Professional beekeepers and scientists from several Western Hemisphere countries are bracing for the most fantastic and potentially dangerous invasions of insects in this century.

A line of defense is being established at the Panama Canal to stop the northward drive of millions of mean and nasty big superbees from Brazil.

The superbees are mutants: the unnatural and unwanted products of an ill-fated and unwise attempt to improve South American honeybees.

In the late 1950's, some South American farmers imported a strain of African bees in order to develop a stronger and more productive species for the local honey industry. Unfortunately, about two dozen bee swarms — with their queens — escaped from the experimental breeding station and flew off into the jungles of southern Brazil.

For the next decade, unnoticed and unchecked in the wild, these African bees interbred with the European-type bees then found in Brazil. The result was a new race of superbees: strong and productive, but also unpredictable, unmanageable, aggressive, and blood-thirsty. Indeed, huge swarms of "Brazilian bees" have been known to attack men and animals without warning or provocation. In some cases, the attacks have been fatal.

The new breed of bee is apparently replacing the milder and more manageable honeybees. Worse yet, they seem to be spreading steadily over South America — and have already crossed the natural barrier of the Amazon. Based on their current rate of spread, this means they should reach Panama before 1980. From there, it's only a short flight to the United States, where experts suspect they could survive as far north as Virginia. Indeed, there is no known geological or climate barrier that could stop the spread of bees in North America.

An international committee has been formed to find ways of halting this northward advance of bees in Central America. Most scientists hope to modify or improve the superbee breed so its strength and honey production can be preserved — but its nastiness eliminated!

Fire and Ice

The Aysen Province of southern Chile is one of the most forbidding and rugged areas of the world. Indeed, this land almost appears as part of another more evil and more terrible planet.

A mixture of towering peaks, dark lifeless valleys, and jagged coastline, this part of Chile resembles the shattered backbone of some crippled giant. Here, as the South American continent reaches out to the Antarctic, the great Andes Mountains fall straight into the sea and the landscape becomes a jumbled mixture of water, rock, and ice.

Few men care — or dare — to tempt nature by living here. The province is as deserted as it is barren. There are no large cities and even few villages. Only rough dirt trails lead up into the few mountain valleys where hardy breeds of both cattle and men live in a constant battle against the elements.

In the summer of 1971, while most Americans enjoyed the last days of sun and surf, the people of the Huemules Valley in Aysen Province were struggling through the last days of the Southern Hemisphere's winter. Their hopes — and, indeed, their very survival — were pinned on the early arrival of spring.

But it was not spring's warmth that would arrive unexpectedly in the Huemules Valley. Instead, it was the burning, searing, killing heat of a volcano.

On August 12, the Hudson Volcano high above the headwaters of the Huemules River erupted violently and without warning, sending a smoke cloud more than 15,000 feet into the air, spewing hot ashes over some 60 square miles of land, and sending rivers of lava pouring down the valley.

For more than a week, eruption after eruption shattered the quiet of the mountains, and a steady stream of red-hot lava flowed over fields and pastures, cutting off roads, damming rivers, and leveling the flimsy stone and wood huts of the simple cattle herders.

More than 10,000 head of cattle and sheep were driven from the valley by the lava, but many others died in the steaming flows. Still other livestock, trapped in canyons and arroyos, slowly starved to death as a thick layer of ashes covered their meager grazing lands.

Government officials and rescue teams were prevented from helping these people — or even inspecting the damage — by poor weather conditions and rugged terrain. In many places people could be evacuated only by helicopter. Unfortunately, high winds and blinding snow squalls grounded aircraft for days after the disaster.

To complicate the problems, the heat of the eruption melted ice and snow on the volcano's slopes and on nearby glaciers, so that avalanches of mud, water, and ice rolled down the steep mountainsides in the wake of the lava flow.

Because the valley is so remote and sparsely populated, the human death toll from the eruption was relatively small. Still, the Smithsonian learned that only a handful of the 50 scattered families living and working in the valley survived.

Some day those few men and women who managed to live through that terrifying week of "fire and ice" may come down from their mountains and tell the rest of the world what it was like to have seen "hell on earth."

Attack of the Killer Whales

For centuries, fishermen have told tales of fantastic battles between deadly killer whales and giant elephant seals. But were these stories true? No one had ever witnessed and confirmed such attacks. Some people claimed they were only myths, similar to the tales of sea serpents and mermaids.

The legend became real life, however, in December 1973, when two American naturalists had front-row seats for a frightening show: the attack and killing of a two-ton elephant seal by two bloodthirsty killer whales.

The two men were floating in a small boat off the coast of Mexico's Baja Peninsula on a bright, sunny afternoon, photographing and recording the hunting and feeding behavior of killer whales.

Suddenly, they noticed a commotion near the shoreline. Two killer whales, one a 20-foot male, the other a 15-foot female, were apparently stalking a huge bull elephant seal.

Like cowboys with a stray steer, the whales circled the clumsy seal, lunging and pushing at it, their jaws snapping, so that the animal was driven from its relatively safe haven in the shallow coastal waters. Slowly, surely, deliberately, the two whales, working as a team, pushed the seal toward open sea and its doom.

Once in deeper waters, the seal was at the mercy of the whales. In a flash, they began their attack.

The bull whale charged the seal and slashed at its soft underbelly. The huge seal bellowed in pain and beat at the water with its ineffectual flippers. Around the wounded animal, the frothing sea quickly turned pink.

While the cow whale waited a distance away,

as if blocking any avenue of escape, the bull whale attacked a second time. Again, the seal was viciously cut.

Still once more the whale attacked. This time, the result was fatal. The mammoth elephant seal, perhaps once a proud and strong leader of a herd, disappeared beneath the waters. The entire attack had taken just a few minutes. Only blood and some tufts of fur remained floating on the surface above the battle zone.

The two naturalists sat stunned in their small skiff. The horrifying battle had taken place before their eyes, without any of the animals paying them the slightest attention.

Perhaps the most chilling part of the battle was its aftermath: The killer whales simply turned from their stricken foe and swam away! They made no attempt to feed on their victim. They had killed out of hate, not hunger. Until the next time, at least, the whales ruled this part of the sea.

Fire in the Lake

The Great Rift Valley slices through East Africa like the track of a giant's plow.

Beginning in the Gulf of Aden, the Rift runs inland, splitting the lowlands of the Somalia Peninsula from the Ethiopian highlands, then turns west and south to create the chain of mountain lakes — Rudolf, Dwania, Albert, Tanganyika, and Nyasa — that feed the Nile and Congo Rivers.

For geologists, the Rift represents a major seam in the armor-plate crust of the Earth. Along this seam, they say, the continent of Africa may be splitting apart, with its two halves drifting off in opposite directions.

While the acutal separation of the African continent is still some eons away, the Rift has created a fantastic landscape of towering cliffs, yawning chasms, fathomless lakes, cascading waterfalls, and spectacular volcanoes.

One of the most spectacular of these is also one of the rarest and most unusual types in the world. Nyragongo is a vast bubbling lake of red-hot lava deep inside a high mountain crater.

Nyrangongo is located north of Lake Kivu in the volcanic range of the Virunga Mountains marking the boundary between Zaire and the tiny African nations of Uganda and Rwanda.

For more than 40 years, this lake of glowing, steaming molten lava has been almost constantly active. Loss of heat at the surface of the lake produces a dark sluggish crust, but the seething molten mass below constantly cracks this ashlike covering so that bright crimson streaks of liquid lava show through.

Nyrangongo is particularly striking at night, when the deep bowl-like crater looks like a devil's cauldron of some fiendish brew.

When the volcano was first discovered 75 years ago, this lava lake was not visible, for the inside of the crater was ringed by a series of overhanging ledges or rims apparently marking the various lava levels of past eruptions.

Even in 1928, when scientists first began systematic surveys of the volcano, no lake could be seen from the wall of the main crater because the lava lay beneath three interior ledges. A bright red glow at night from the bowels of the mountain gave unmistakable evidence of its presence, however.

But the nature of Nyrangongo has changed dramatically in the past 20 years. Particularly since 1965, when the lava lake changed from a tiny molten pool deep at the crater bottom to the present vast lake covered with a cool crust.

The lava lake is still rising steadily and rapidly — sometimes as much as several feet in a few hours.

Most interesting, perhaps, the lake now seems to grow by lava from below forcing its way through fissures and cracks in the crust to cool on top.

Before the crust formed in 1965, the entire column of lava seemed to rise and fall together, pushed up from below. Now, in a manner of speaking, the lake is growing from the top down.

Various expeditions visit Nyrangongo each year to study the phenomenon first-hand. Volcanic activity permitting, some scientists actually camp inside the main crater on a natural platform only 700 feet above the boiling lava.

For several weeks at a time, these researchers make extensive temperature, pressure, and heat measurements as part of the program to chart Nyrangongo's long-term ups and downs.

The goal of this and other research efforts at this fantastic volcano is to develop a better understanding of volcanic activity, so that someday in the future man may be able to predict more accurately the next time a mountain will blow its top.

The Star-Struck Feline

On the night of October 27, 1973, a calico cat named Misty joined an extremely small and exclusive fraternity of earthly creatures who have been hit by falling stars.

That evening a meteorite crashed through the roof of a garage two miles north of Canon City, Colorado, penetrated the interior ceiling, and shattered upon hitting the concrete floor.

Misty, catnapping behind a pile of old furniture in a corner of the garage, was slightly bruised by chunks of the flying cosmic debris.

More than three pounds of meteoritical material, including 50 pebble-sized pieces, as well as many smaller fragments and dust, were recovered from the garage floor. The meteorite was identified by Smithsonian scientists as a stony type.

The hole in the roof and ceiling of the garage indicated the meteorite had fallen almost straight down. No one in the area could report seeing a bright fireball or hearing noises associated with the fall.

Incidents of meteorites striking buildings — or even landing near inhabited areas of the world — are rare. Before 1968, no more than one or two cases had been reported every 10 years. But since the Center for Short-Lived Phenomena has been established, more incidents have been noted.

For example, earlier in 1973 a small meteorite plummeted through the roof of a trailer carport in California. Just two years before that, another meteorite crashed through the roof and imbedded itself in the living-room ceiling of a Wethersfield, Connecticut, home.

In 1971, a meteorite containing microscopic particles of diamondlike material hit a storehouse in Finland. And a 1969 meteorite that fell into a barn at Murchison, Australia, turned out to be a scientific bonanza. That rock was easily and quickly recovered by farmers who saw it fall almost at their feet. It contained the first confirmed traces of organic molecules.

A veritable rain of meteorites — some 2,000 pounds in all — fell on houses of the little Mexican town of Pueblito de Allende in 1969. Small boys collected rocks from roofs and rain spouts to sell to space scientists and rock hounds.

Still, the meteorite fall at Canon City is extraordinary, for it is only the second known time a living creature has been struck by extraterrestrial material.

Misty the Cat joins company with a lady in Alabama who, 20 years before, was bopped by a meteorite that tore through the roof of her house, bounced off a bureau, and struck her while she lay asleep on a divan.

The Poisoned Sheep

Even the crusty old shepherd nearly broke into tears when he looked at the hillside. Strewn among the rock and sagebrush, in all directions as far as the eye could see, lay countless small white clumps of wool. Half his herd of sheep were dead — victims of a mysterious and silent killer.

When more than 1,250 sheep were found dead in a mountain pasture near Garrison, Utah, in 1972, the immediate reaction of most local residents was stark fear. Garrison is downwind from the U.S. Army's Dugway Proving Ground, where the newest and most deadly kinds of poison gas are developed and tested.

Could the sheep have been killed by nerve gas escaping from these test laboratories? And, worse yet, would the residents of Garrison be the next victims?

Perhaps the fears of Garrison were justified. Scattered cases of death and sickness caused by spills of bacteriological and radioactive materials have been only too well known in this country in the last 30 years.

This time, however, Garrison — and all America — would be lucky. The sheep were not gassed by a new secret weapon — they had been killed by one of nature's own equally lethal and secretive poisons.

Unknowingly, the sheep had fed on a toxic weed known as *halogeton*. This low, red, prickly plant contains unusual amounts of moisture; thus, it is particularly attractive to sheep. Unfortunately, it is also deadly! In the digestive system of the sheep, the weed turns into fast-acting poison. (Ironically, cattle can eat the same weed without any ill effects.)

Half the herd had apparently wandered into a

section of range where this killer weed made up some 60 percent of the vegetation. The other half of the herd grazed on a different hillside less than a mile away and survived.

Indeed, it was the survival of the other sheep that made investigators doubt poison gas as a cause of death. The gas would have killed every living creature in its path — including the people of Garrison.

The Violent Birth

Karua, one of the South Pacific's newest islands, is growing into a healthy young adult and scientists around the world are relieved to find their baby is living so long.

The tiny world of Karua was born in a spasm of volcanic violence; and, like any proud and worried parents, marine biologists and volcanologists waited apprehensively to see if this new addition would survive the terrible pains of its delivery.

On Washington's Birthday, 1971, the submarine volcano Karua blasted up from the sea floor less than five miles from the island Epi in the New Hebrides Archipelago northeast of Australia.

Throughout most of that first day, the sea bubbled and churned around Karua as ashes spewed from beneath the sea. A cloud of smoke rose more than 3,000 feet over the volcano. Several times each minute, explosions shattered the quiet of the blue Pacific and hurled massive boulders high in the air.

The following morning, after the smoke and dust and steam had cleared away, scientists on nearby islands could see waves lapping against a black cinder pile nearly 600 feet long, 200 feet wide, and several feet high.

Two days later, a small group of adventurous scientists took a motor launch out to the still warm island. The strange black barren landscape, dotted with craters and cracked with volcanic vents, looked like a section of the moon.

In most scientific catalogs, Karua was listed only as a "volcanic area." Under normal conditions, the cone of Karua lay submerged and dormant beneath the surface, its location marked only by a lighter shade of ocean blue.

Yet, twice before in recent history — once at

the turn of the century and again in the late 1940's — Karua had erupted and created similar islands. In 1901, it produced an island almost a mile long. In 1948, a volcanic cone over a mile in diameter protruded some 300 feet from the ocean. Neither island lasted more than a year.

The lava produced by oceanic volcanoes is usually a frothy, porous, and extremely fragile material — certainly not suited to withstand the battering of waves or even the constant flow of gentle currents.

Three years before, a similar island had bubbled out of the sea after a volcanic eruption several hundred miles east of Karua. Metis Shoals lasted only a few months.

At that time, a Smithsonian scientist, Dr. Charles Lundquist, traveling to Australia took a quick detour to investigate Metis Shoals before it disappeared. Dr. Lundquist returned to Washington with a suitcase full of crumbly gray rock, which is today the only proof that Metis Shoals ever existed.

Fortunately, scientists now have more than that to show from Karua! The bleak little lava pile seems determined to remain alive and well above the water.

Given enough time and the right conditions, windblown seeds and spores could take root on Karua and create a full-fledged, permanent member of the New Hebrides island chain.

The Sad Saga of Suzie

For nearly a month and a half in the summer of 1973, whale lovers around the world rooted for Suzie, the sole survivor of a beaching incident that killed eight other members of her herd.

On June 13th, nine pilot whales stranded themselves on Grassy Key, about seven miles northeast of Marathon, Florida. Eight were dead. But one whale — a 6-foot-long, 500-pound young female — was found alive, floundering in shallow waters offshore, by members of the Florida Marine Patrol.

Repeated efforts to tow the surviving whale into deep water were unsuccessful. She seemed determined to head back onto the beach and die with her companions. In desperation, the men finally towed the young whale to a nearby boat basin where she was found to have serious sunburns covering her entire back. She was immediately coated with lanolin to reduce blistering and fed antibiotics to prevent infection.

Six days later, this whale — by now dubbed "Suzie" by her many new friends — was moved to the Flipper Sea School at Marathon. Here she was treated by a veterinarian and tube-fed a diet of minced fish and shrimp bolstered with vitamins and antibiotics. Within a week, her burns closed and healed without any infection and Suzie seemed to be in good physical condition.

Throughout the next month, marine biologists carefully watched Suzie's recovery. The rest of the world watched as well, for Suzie was setting new records for survival in captivity.

Pilot whales are also called "Atlantic blackfish," and males may grow to a length of 18 feet. The species is well known in East Coast waters, particularly for their strange and unexplained tendency to ram themselves up on beaches. Unfortunately, the skin of the pilot whale is particularly sensitive to the sun and quickly blisters when out of water. Also, they are unable to get rid of body heat effectively (they can't perspire like human beings), so beached whales die rapidly. None has ever survived for more than a few days after being rescued.

For a while, it seemed Suzie might be the exception. But then in July, 45 days after she had been rescued from the shallow waters of Grassy Key, Suzie died.

For three days before her death she did not accept her special food and medicine mixture. Still, she did not appear to be suffering. In fact, Suzie had played actively in the large natural pool at the Flipper Sea School and fed on live snapper until the night before her death.

An autopsy indicated Suzie had died from a severe case of pneumonia that had been unnoticed by her helpers. Without her daily supply of antibiotics, her unsuspected lung condition had worsened and finally caused her death.

Ironically, Suzie was found in the shallowest end of the pool. As death approached, she apparently tried to "beach" herself again.

The Slipping Earth

Thousands of years ago, before even the native American Indian crossed the continent, vast areas of Quebec were covered by the waters of a great inland sea that now has shrunk to become Lake Champlain. As those waters evaporated and the sea dried up, a deep layer of soft clay was left in its place.

This clay was a very unstable material, about the same composition as the fine, soft silt found on today's ocean floors. In fact, when exposed to water again, this clay would quickly liquify and return to its original gummy, mucky state.

Nine thousand years later, man built a vast housing development on that clay base. Row after row of small white one-story ranch-type houses lined perfectly straight and parallel streets above the ancient sea bed.

Of course, few residents of the modern town of St. Jean-Vianney, Quebec, knew the ancient history of their town. And none could have guessed they would one day be victims of geological processes that had begun eons earlier.

The spring of 1971 in Quebec had been unusually long and wet. Heavy winter snows had led to equally heavy spring runoffs from the rivers and streams of Canada's northern woods. The Petit Bras River that flowed past the town was running high and fast and a number of small landslips had occurred along its banks in April.

Then late on the morning of May 4, while most housewives in St. Jean-Vianney were sitting down with a second cup of coffee, the bottom fell out of their town — and their lives!

Houses, cars, toys, playgrounds, gardens, garages, pets, and people suddenly dropped into a muddy wet pit; whirling, spinning, and turning in the debris; tumbling and churning with rocks, trees, and sections of lawn. The horrible sounds of wood splintering and stones crushing mingled with the terrified cries of mothers and children caught in the horrible downward plunge.

Then all was silent.

A huge, 350,000-square-yard section of St. Jean-Vianney had dropped 100 feet and then slid nearly a half mile down a slope and into the Petit Bras River. Over 50 houses were destroyed. More than 40 people were killed, scores more were injured seriously.

The ancient inland sea — dry for centuries before any man ever trod its shores — had returned to its original slippery, unstable state. Nine thousand years after it had evaporated and dried up, it was still claiming victims!

The Survivors

In an age of endangered species, hatch failures, and fish kills, isn't it nice to know that some species are surviving — and even thriving?

For example, 1973 was a banner year for butterflies. Throughout the autumn, East Coast residents watched seemingly endless streams of Monarch butterflies winging south. This peak year in the complex cycle of butterfly reproduction provided a rare thrill for butterfly collectors.

An even rarer phenomenon occurred in the preceding spring when millions of "Painted Lady" butterflies were observed over Colorado. For several days, the skies over Denver were filled with butterflies circling aimlessly without any sense of direction. Then, one morning as if on signal, the entire colorful flotilla flew off together northward.

Not all insect outbreaks are as beautiful as butterfly migrations, however. The northeastern United States continues to be plagued by hordes of the forest-destroying gypsy moths. Also, millions of odd-looking insects known as "walking sticks" infest the Knobley Mountains of West Virginia, defoliating vast areas of black locust and hackberry trees. And Massachusetts was recently visited by the hemlock looper, a hungry inchworm which chewed up acres of forest north of Boston.

Across the ocean in Belgium, oak, buckthorn, and hawthorn, plus many apple and pear trees, were stripped of their leaves and fruits by an army of brown-tail caterpillars. Although each caterpillar is only slightly longer than an inch, a colony of thousands can strip an entire tree bare of foliage overnight.

The Belgian caterpillar outbreak ended on a

happy note, however, because the bugs provided food for flocks of birds, especially the European cuckoo.

Apparent disasters sometimes do produce unexpected and beneficial side effects. The severe Mississippi floods of 1973 destroyed millions of dollars of property, but they also produced a bumper crop of red crayfish.

Crayfish are able to survive long periods of drought and extremely cold temperatures by "hibernating" in sealed burrows under the mud. The flood apparently awakened those crayfish lying dormant since the last high water.

Crayfish, of course, are important ingredients in such popular Creole dishes as jambalaya and "crawfish pie." But the little crustaceans are also a delicacy for many fish, birds, and bullfrogs living in the Mississippi Basin. In fact, the unexpected abundance of crayfish after the flood may have helped thousands of raccoons, trapped on islands by high water, survive starvation.

Finally, the most positive note on the survival of the species came from the tiny Penikese Island off the coast of Massachusetts. In the spring of 1973, the Audubon Society spotted a pair of Manx shearwaters, members of the puffin family, nesting there.

Although the Manx shearwaters are great long-distance wanderers over the Atlantic, they normally nest in Europe and this was the first recorded nesting on the North American continent.

More important, the nest's single egg hatched successfully, thus marking the first known birth of such a bird in the United States.

Could this be the start of another population explosion?

Stone Age Meets Space Age

While American astronauts toured the lunar landscape in their own "space sports car" during the summer of 1971, a team of scientists in the Philippine Islands discovered a forgotten tribe of primitive people who had never seen an ocean, never tasted salt, rice, or sugar, and who had never even heard of tobacco *let alone astronauts!*

First contact between the civilized world and the lost Tasaday people came on June 7, 1971, when a helicopter carrying an exploration team from the Philippine National Museum touched down in a small clearing high on a forested mountainside on rugged Mindanao Island.

Led into the forest by a native trader named Dafal, the anthropologists found a tiny band of 24 people who survived solely by trapping small animals and gathering wild plants and fruits.

The Tasadays had no knowledge of rice, sweet potatos, corn, cassava, or any other cultivated plants. Indeed, they didn't even have words in their language for this type of food!

They had never tasted salt and sugar or smoked tobacco. (At first, the tribe refused gifts of salt and sugar, thinking them poisonous, but the small children quickly developed a taste for candy. No one, however, could be persuaded to smoke!)

The Tasadays still used stone tools — mainly flat, sharp rocks used as simple scrapers to make pointed bamboo spears and knives. Only four metal tools were found among the Tasadays, and all of these had been given to them by the trader Dafal during the past five years.

Living in almost total social and geographical isolation, the Tasadays apparently had no formal trade or any contacts with anyone from the outside world except Dafal. Still, they seemed to know that other people lived around them, sometimes hearing the voices of hunters in the forest. A few of the braver Tasadays had even seen the fields and houses of the "strange people" who lived in the lowlands "near where the sun sets." Yet, the Tasadays had no words to describe or name other people and their own language seemed only loosely related to other Philippine tongues.

The entire world of the Tasadays was enclosed within the dense, cloud-shrouded mountain forests where they are born, live, and die. Because their universe exists under these trees, they have no words for lakes, oceans, open fields, constellations, or phases of the moon.

In fact, for the Tasadays, "heaven" existed in the tops of the trees. It was there that they went after death; and their ancestors "watched" them from the upper branches.

Rumors of these lost people had filtered down from other tribes living on the edges of the thick mountain forests. Members of the Manubo Blit tribe who hunt wild boar and deer with bow-and-arrow traps told of seeing an unknown people in the forest and finding campsites where animals had been butchered.

It was one of these native trappers — Dafal — who first met the Tasadays. When he found them, by accident, they had no cloth, no metal tools, and not even a bow and arrow. Their only garments were large orchid leaves or strips of beaten tree bark tied about their waists with string.

Over several years of visiting the Tasadays, Dafal brought them metal bolo knives, cloth, bows, and a few feet of brass wire from which they made earrings.

The Tasadays live amid some of the most isolated and rugged land in the Philippine Archipelago, yet only a 30-minute helicopter ride from a fairly large development at Kemato. The tribe lives along the headwaters of the scores of small rivers and streams that begin high in the mountains and cut narrow twisting lanes through hundreds of miles of dark, damp forests.

The land is as hostile and inhospitable as it looks, with resources so limited that only a small number of Tasadays can be supported. Probably no more than 100 Tasadays exist in several small, loosely related, and widely scattered "bands," or family groups.

The basic diet of these people consists of wild yams and fruits, as well as some crabs, fish, and large tadpoles found in the streams.

If life is hard for the Tasadays, it is also short. The scientists found no elderly men and women among the group they met. Sickness, especially the type of disease brought in from the outside, wipes out the old and weak quickly.

In fact, when asked what they feared most,

the Tasadays didn't say evil spirits, or wild animals, or other tribes, or even the strange aircraft that they must see flying over their forest homes. The most dreaded thing in their lives is *fugu* — epidemic sickness. With good reason! A disease like cholera — or even influenza — could destroy the Tasadays overnight, for they have no natural resistance to the germs of civilization.

This fear of disease — and the unconscious knowledge that it comes from outside — has made the Tasadays hide away from the world for centuries.

The Tasadays could not have hidden much longer. Their forest home is rapidly being invaded by homesteading farmers, loggers, and ranchers. Contact — possibly violent — between the Tasadays and civilization was inevitable. Fortunately, the anthropologists arrived first. Fortunate for *both* the Tasadays — and us!

The Philippine officials hope to protect the Tasadays by the establishment of large forest reserves in the mountains. Here the Tasadays will be allowed to remain unchanged if they choose.

By good management of the new agricultural and lumbering activities on the land around these mountain reserves, the government hopes to protect the environment. These border areas of controlled development may also provide opportunities to train and educate the Tasadays for their changing role in the modern world.

At the same time, the Tasadays may have much to teach modern man. Already research teams are with the Tasadays in the forest attempting to answer many questions about their lives. How can they survive without farming, metals, or permanent homes? What foods do they find free and wild in the forests? How much food is necessary to survive as a tribe? And how long can the group survive in one area before it must move to another?

The Tasadays provide a rare opportunity for 20th-century man to observe first-hand how his primitive ancestors lived. As true hunters and food-gatherers who still live off the land, the Tasadays offer a living demonstration of how man once existed in perfect harmony with his environment — indeed, as an integral part of the total ecological system.

The Falling Fishes

A very strange rainfall over Australia's Northern Territory in February 1974 had ichthyologists as well as meteorologists scratching their heads. That's right, *ichthyologists* — those scientists who study fish — joined the Aussie weathermen in trying to explain why hundreds of small fish fell from the skies over a desolate area of the so-called "outback," miles away from any water.

Bill Tapp, a rugged rancher who runs the sprawling Killarney cattle station (or ranch) near the remote settlement of Katherine, reported that several hundred fish, all about two to three inches in length, had rained down on his land.

Rancher Tapp claimed the fabulous fish falls occurred during a violent tropical storm associated with the annual autumn rains. (Remember, the seasons are reversed "down under"!)

Scores of fish fell near Tapp's ranch house, creating the odd and unbelievable sight of tiny silver fish flopping about in the dust and dirt of a normally parched desertlike land.

Officials at the Australian weather bureau speculate that the fish deluge may have resulted from a weird combination of tornado and thunderstorm, not at all uncommon in this part of the country at that time of the year.

Such a frightening combination often creates waterspouts over the sea. These whirlwinds are powerful enough to suck up water, seaweed, bits of driftwood, and even whole schools of fish floating near the surface.

These strong winds may then blow this watery mixture of flotsam and jetsam inland to fall on unsuspecting farmers, aborigines, and kangaroos strolling through the otherwise dry and barren scrublands of the "outback."

Weather watchers in Darwin, Australia, claim that cases of falling fish are fairly regular occurences in the Northern Territory and Queensland. In fact, Rancher Bill Tapp didn't seem too concerned about the finny rainfall in his backyard. When the Center for Short-Lived Phenomena asked him for more information about this unusual downpour of fish, he replied simply: "They look like perch."

Perhaps in that upside-down land, where the seasons are backward, and the everyday animals are kangaroos and kuala bears, dingos and duckbilled platypuses, the unusual becomes commonplace and the oddball is oftentimes old hat.